The Foreclosure

The Foreclosure

Poems by
Richard Emil Braun

University of Illinois Press
Urbana, Chicago, London

Acknowledgments: *Salmagundi*, "Listening"; *Modern Poetry Studies*, "Ties That Bind," and "Against Nature"; *Prism*, "An Unknown Friend" and "Niagara"; *Fresco*, "The Power" and "Austin Gothic"; *Triad*, "Hunger"; *Accent*, "Spano"; *Quagga*, "New Day," "Mosh," "Faith," and "Palms"; *The Minnesota Review*, "The Oil." "Black and Midnight Blue," "Spano," "New Day," "Mosh," "Faith," "Santa Monica," and "Palms" appeared as No. 1 of the Fresco Chapbook Series under the title *Companions to Your Doom*, 1961 (edition limited to 500 copies).

The President's Medal of the University of Western Ontario was awarded in 1965 for "Niagara" as the best poem to appear in a Canadian magazine during the previous year.

In memoriam

A.A.B.
M.M.B.

Contents

One

Listening

Be you alone in essence or circumstance.
    The bottle may be full
  or dry. Insomnia is not
        prerequisite.

The you we regard will be listening
    to heartbeat then beyond
  to the breath of adjacent rooms
        and of outdoors

(much as this you or I often listens
    to strangers articulate
  if either this you or I falls
        inarticulate)

and to what breath is imminent not next door,
    not outside, not from you,
  you listen most attentively.
        As for your heart,

waiting on it has come to bore you by now.
    Fear has arrived; changed shape;
  and there remains dim attentiveness
        as though upon

a guest who will tell you his whole sad story.
    You are listening beyond.
  Was there a fluffy moth? Is it
        a visitor?

Let me warn you, Louella, to spare you pain:
    Mirrors exist which, if
  you're a colored man (which I, for one,
        am not) pull you

into like a cigar or press you into
a semblance of the surface
of a cup of coffee (add cream
to make your shade)

and if this can happen to a colored
man, to a dead man what
cannot? Mostly, at death, they emerge
with ease through mouth,

nose, or you know where, and are replicas,
the ghostly body (flimsy
as it is compared to the flesh)
undistorted;

sometimes, and this is common, they blow (like
cirri) through a sudden
crevice or strain through a suture
(as through a grating)

and are grotesques. So be ready, Louella,
as you squat listening,
for the possibilities of sight
as well; for like

the gentle snake that has no eyelids but
that bravely harks with its
quick tongue to anything, you shall
have to see too.

While you wait, I approach. I am destined
not to come to you in time.
I slouch in the alley watching
the caged white lights

of the fire escape opposite yours.
    In the bar I decided:
  "Now she will be encountering
      the foreclosure

on perceptivity, on sloppy kindness,
    on habits of silence.
  Let it come to her. It's hers only.
      My love will accept

her pain, not her experience." The smell of
    the bar, that of urine,
  reminds me of jail as I meet
      the outdoor air.

Now I climb your fire escape. You huddle
    in your blanket (a hot bath
  shall have failed to soothe you) and watch
      white spiders hustle

in their shadows on the wall. It is dark
    in the hall. I shuffle
  slowly. Below me (is it in
      a room?) I hear

some humans (or underfoot?) and I stop.
    To you, to the you we
  regard, meanwhile, there comes a breath,
      and a visitant

rises, gathered of fog, vague, approaching
    in loops, gesticulating,
  its left eye swelling and its right
      withdrawing with

the effort to concentrate, at last mumbles
    like one who talks in sleep,
then disperses. You are unmoved.
        In the hall I wait

too long scrupling (will I stomp a naked
    hand with the next step?) and
listen to courses of tongues and teeth
        begetting bruises

and more (who knows?) with a gelatinous
    melody of the inner
thighs. I jump, turn, and (as I said,
        too late) find your door.

You crouch, dumb. Your never-blinking eyes are
    fixed. You turn your head in
order not to be forced to see
        my eyes. Though I now

(who have come to seize your pain, whatever
    its cause, and to disperse it
within myself, whatever the
        consequences)

understand that the clamp of my hand is
    (to you now) the world groping
for where to enter and corrode you,
        I must persist;

and having only my hands and voice to reach
    you with, I handle teats
and shrinking shoulders and stop it,
        and I explain

("It was the dust of a moth, the breath of
    a ghost") and exhort ("What
of wind and fluff while your choice body
    beats and breathes?") But you

are bored of listening to your heart beat, to me,
    and beyond; and as I brag
("You'll never see some of yourself,
    Louella, as so

fine as reflected in my eyes") I guess
    (in this projection of
the future, which is my fear) that you
    are not hurt by thirst

or loneliness or what appeared; and seeing
    that tears are drizzling
off your face, I know they are for me,
    for my, my pain.

The Power

You're naturally good enough, I said, Too good is the trouble.
But the gift and calling might not hold you back from falling.
"But you lose what you have when you bury what's been
                                                    bestowed,"
    she says (which I knew she would say). I decided
to bring her to my mother-in-law to speak some sense to her.
    But since then I've had more matters to think over.

Think about every widow that opens a mournful chapel
in her living room. Thing to do. Like seven or two colored
and five foreigner ladies there. Altar's an old-time school platform.
    I see a young man in a foreign uniform,
she tells all the foreigner ladies because every one has lost
    a son. That's the kind of reading they give at best.

Sometimes it's not that way, I know. I tell her, You'd be real,
but the power of music and the power of money
are massed against you, Honey. I know you can really cure.
    Others try the same, and they also are sincere.
Dusty rooms and empty stores. These women are always losing.
    And consider, I tell her, The way you've been dreaming.

You dream you're on your knees. Around you millions of rats
                                                    crawl.
To dream you're on your knees means you need help. Rats are
                                                    betrayers.
No one can purely depend on prayers. But you give a number:
    you'll heal and read, and you'll succeed. No one can want more.
(At this time we were walking close to my mother-in-law's.)
    She says: "It's prayer alone where all real power lies.

Let others do it. Telling numbers is not spiritual."
My mother-in-law reads magazines. She's a settled lady
and seldom works. She reads. So we went in and asked her what
    she thought. She said she read where recently a white
Reverend prayed over a patch of beans. The beans he prayed for
    grew one third faster than the others. "There you are,"

my friend said. That night I told my husband. He said Big deal.
This man says that man said that, that man says this man said
                                                    this,
he said, That's all the information we have. Going to be
    prosperity, there's going to be equality,
there's going to be war, he said, You can throw it on the floor.
    Those were the first new things I had to think over.

The next I learned at work. I work for very rich people.
They have two sons. One son has an English car. He does nothing
but run with women. He's thin. But the other one will sit
    at home all day, quaffs whiskey and reads thick books. He's fat.
He said he read where a doctor in India had a man
    play a flute in a cornfield, and in that field the corn

grew thirty-five percent faster. Truth is universal,
whoever says it, drunk or not. I tell that to my friend.
I say: Sunday morning trucks cruise broadcasting sacred songs.
    They huckster big churches where there's music and things
that go with music: Princes of the church in gold-cloth gowns
    with buttons of pearl like saxophones, and saxophones

of gold with pearl buttons. Go to a big, singing Temple
to be enriched and cured. You won't be cured, my husband says,
You'll just be less afraid. Your summer Sundays, nothing to do;
    stand on the stoop in underwear; sniff barbeque
from yards and dead rats on the asphalt; watch the funerals
    (them sticking blue flags on the cars); hear boys and girls.

My friend is going to open a meditative chapel.
She says she dreams of children now, which means success. I say
the thing to do first is let the persons that ought discern just
   what the power that grows and heals is. Have a contest,
I say, between all kinds of preacher and various music,
   in a guarded greenhouse, perfectly scientific,

under government supervision. Till we know, you're a fool,
I tell her, to act alone. My husband tells her Go ahead.
Get the money. Get that money. She pays us no attention.
   Sunday he says Let's all go to the park, have fun.
So we three go, have fried fish and drink pop. We sleep on rugs.
   We can hear rats or something crackling sandwich bags.

An Unknown Friend

'I wonder, do you think there is something unnatural
    about my boy, the way he dreams
  alone in the yard? He ought to be glad
    to play with the other children.

You have a little girl. What is your opinion?'
    "Figure it's just a stage," the second
  lady says—she an American. "They go
    through periods, but they quickly pass."

(A birdbath with a bambino nuzzling a porpoise
    stands nearby; beyond it peonies
  bloom, red—'as red cabbage' the foreign lady
    described them—and white; and over

the highest, in its wheel web with azure signature,
    a great golden-garden-spider waits.)
  'I had believed,' the first says, 'that by that age,
    past four, a boy would mould the whole world

with his hands to make the world a thing which a child
    can use—the way you squeeze a lump
  of clay until it fits to your fingers.'
    And the other woman says "I asked

our pediatrician. He thought if it doesn't last
    too long it's normal if they dream.
  They model themselves a mental world before
    they can handle the actual one.

When your boy learns more English he'll have lots more fun.
    Oh dear! Look at that big spider."
  (This is an early-vernal noon, too warm:
    a fantasy pause we have between

rains and that final muddy freeze of Michigan
    that clenches summer blissfully—
as though there had never been any snowfall
    in May, or disillusionment.)

The first says 'Yes. A spider waits; web with slight
                  movement . . .
    like what I fear. My boy will shiver
in the yard and watch the fence but doesn't
    see the fence. He sees beyond it,

he says, where his friend is hiding. I ask him what
    his friend is. He pretends not to know.
But where the sweet pea vine and honeysuckle
    join, he says he sees a swishing wall,

as of strings, and just past that, just sometimes there will
    be a kind of magic playmate
whom he can see a tiny bit by moving
    from side to side without moving

his eyes. I am afraid. There may be really something
    that wants him. I wish my man were here.'
"I don't know," the second says, "how I could
    manage it, alone in your shoes . . .

Look how those flowers are opening. Figure they'll freeze . . .
    You shouldn't worry. I think a girl
gets to be a girl quicker and simpler
    than a boy a boy." 'Yes. I think too,

each year,' the first says, 'that they will die. They
                seldom do. . . .
    Look at that boy with the fish! Today
I asked my boy if he'd like a dog. I thought
    he would refuse. He said *yes* instead.

14

Then I told him, Someday you will wish to be married.
You should have a girl friend already.
I have. I asked Where? *Where I was when I was
still dead before I was born,* he said.'

Austin Gothic

In blossomy night we, close and slow
and solicitous, strolled
like mirror-image cripples with two good limbs
to share between two.

We saw the house with ivy-spun,
great spreading oak before it,
and, watching the single gable, approached
it, arm in arm.

I said: There's a thing up there, stooped,
its arms held up as in fear
of having its head hit. "Something like a man,
like us rough-cut,"

you said, "pivoting in the attic
among lumber and trunks
and a tattered farthingale." We two fled
and found an oblique

mesquite to sit in, which awful wind
moved and filled with lilac.
One of us spoke, to be helpful. In the bent
tree's thorns air screamed.

That too would scream if it could. We guessed
the mouth is missing. But
it shuffles and gropes and bumps the boarded
window with its wrist.

Hunger

With a tic, with canine gusto, Dirty Eddie,
    bearded, bulging in corduroy,
        tells me of his "entremets" . . .
    What is this to you and to me, girl?
I wrangle perforce with hideous relevancies
    to our banquet of affection,
  just as I choke the emetic provisos
    of a planet's inconsistency.
      It is because I must
    deny for a time our separate
two deaths in order in turn to deny our unique
    demise, the sterile arroyo between

your and my abortifacient skin. Your hunger
    has been my royal joy. And often
      enough, away outdoors
    or home with six superfluous
windows blowing, we have thought we had vanished
    in safety into the wide throat
  of an enemy. As often as well
    we have rendered ourselves mutual
      to our lips and tongues, and have
    felt then, fools, that we were fed on our
single body of affection and needed never
    hence mumble a nipple of soil or knead

the planet's brambled groin. . . . I am in a city now,
    a minor city with small bush by,
      remembering greater woods
    maybe you remember with me.
You by your Gulf of Mexico, and I fake lord
    of porcupines by Georgian Bay,
    were close. We stay as close today as ever
    our skins' breadth allowed us to be.

How are you? Where are you, girl?
I cannot journey home just now.
Why should I while the julep of memory lasts?
The inimical world will produce, soon,

a raw coating of albuminous snow shot red
with traffic lights and tails of cars.
An odor tells us this.
It spices beer, bites voices clear.
I hear a woman sing: *Come and sit by my side*
Hm-hm Hm-hm, and a man turns
and speaks: "You have been in north country. Something
makes me think of those foamy flapjacks
they fix you in the birch
and poplar bush there. Something about
tonight reminds me of them." *But remember the Red . . .*
Yes, so it does, I say. Up there white pine

used to stand so abundant the old loggers
left many they couldn't drag lie,
of a size you'll never find
today anywhere. The man says:
"You step on one of those, you crumble through to the top
of your thigh. So swampy now. Flies
nip your hide. Cedars grow clear from the slough
and top the cliffs. You strip a poplar
twelve feet long. I think you
can dip it down near the shore there
in the shallows till your hands are wet. Hard, sandy
bottom I think is that deep in loon shit."

What death ends has no end. The man leaves. The song stops.
And soon it is Dirty Eddie, drunk,
who turns and tells me things. . . .
But there is time beforehand for me

to poke my memory of us toward my memory
        of your face, in the world to the south.
    Once when forsythia was shedding, gilding
        morsels of dirt, I stood awaiting
            you. I observed the action
        of sovereign earth. Alone, I feared it:
The abdominous spider bounds sideways in a groove
    of mortar on a red wall. On the sidewalk,

the dried body of a dead bee bright as topaz
        against cement tilts in the wind
            of a passing stride as though
        to rise. Just then you came to me.
I drove a hundred miles to the Huron shore.
        You worked my neck. Rain licked the car.
    The close space filled with savor of yourself.
        When day came we treaded wet sands,
            limbering the newest
        bruises of the concussion of our
isodynamic loves. There, soon, we met a bittern
    hen with circular amber eye, standing

in a centimeter of water on one leg,
        her neck retired like a man's
            on a cold day then shot straight,
        fishing minnows with plunges like
a ladle's. We stared. She showed us no fear. Then you
        dove on your knees to me. . . . "The snow,"
    says Dirty Eddie, "will keep them fresh on
        the streets." I say Shut up. But I
            am forced to fight bitter
        similitudes. Hard working, "solid
citizen," but a mad and moon-eyed peasant, Eddie
    claims to be the pretender to the throne

of Hungary. He twitches as he talks. He tells
　　how, reptant, he lurks about parks
　　　in darkness and hearkens
　　　to lovers' hefty music, then sifts
the brush for what he calls "the peels." He shows me a
　　plastic soup-straw. I leave the bar.
　　This is a restaurant. . . . Well, what of it, girl?
　　　I wrestle like a fool with what
　　　I know. I know to deny
　　our sterile unique death I must
for a time accept, above all things, our two deaths;
　　for these will, least of all things, separate.

Near me, habitues chat. "Ever see a guy
　　with the death-hunger on?" says one. What
　　　on? "Know Jack?" Salt of the earth.
　　"Seen Jack, always a light eater,
come in here, eat eat eat, one night; he couldn't fill
　　himself. That same night he was dead.
　　Call that the death-hunger." I shall come home, girl.
　　　Who knows who lives there now? I'll wait.
　　　It will be raining, in our
　　South, like spring. I'll be the real king
who nourishes and does not need you; drenches, fills;
　　who will feed the living our twin dooms bring.

Two

Black and Midnight Blue

Inside, you learn the innocent: who they are,
    what do they wear.
Three colors are allowed. Most wear the grey, many
  a midnight blue, and only I wear black.
    I think I am innocent.
    My black goes greenish here like humus
      in the shade. I think
    black is innocent also. I know

that innocence can injure, but not competently.
    To think of midnight blue, I don't
    consider the warders around,
    I think of somebody who taught me
      philosophy.
  I don't know where he is. His name was Mosh.
    For black, beside myself, I think
      of young Spano.

Where does it start? A cold wind from the south?
    A Spirit winding
its winding way? It starts with German words, I say,
  like *Weltregierung* and *Weltanschauung*.
    I'd like to make a handy
    third word, by your leave, and let that
      be *Weltmoder*,
    the World Mildew, the scene you see.

It starts when Mr. Chinless and Gentian Violet
    walk in the toilet. Gentian Violet
    dangles a baseball bat, and Chinless
    has a derby hat on. And Gentian
      Violet says Man,
  take off your hat. Chinless takes that hat off,
    and Gentian Violet hits him on
      the head. And Chinless

says Why'd you do that, man? And Gentian Violet
         says, Man, why'd you take
your hat off? Well, there's the story that the grey ones tell.
   There's truth in grey, the halfway innocent.
            A virtuous type can
       finally disbelieve in Hell.
            Spano, Mosh: I pray
       for both each day but without good cheer.

I am not courageous concerning the evil
       in the innocent, but I hope;
       and I see, in the innocence
       of the evil, frailty and doom.
            To lie you must
   believe in truth, as Mosh did, as I do,
       as these prisoners believe. Here's
            their newspaper.

   Here's an example. *We are regretful,*
            it reads, *To report*
   that jovial Gerald A. V. Knox known to all
       and sundry as "The Arkansas Traveller"
            passed on the other day.
         Genial "Arkansas" always had
              a cheerful word
       and helping hand for all his friends.

We are all at a loss to surmise who did such
       a lousy thing. The truth is, Gerry
       was a rat. Everyone knew that,
       and I believe most everyone
            in grey connived
   at killing him. Some have confessed it to me:
       Tito and Tutti and Swamp Fox.
            To Hell with them.

Spano, if anyone is innocent,
          was innocent.
He never knew of truth. He knew velleity.
    I met him only a few times; the first
          was in New York, the last
        Detroit. I followed him all night.
            He lifted glasses
      from bars, cans of crab-meat and puny

World War surplus sweaters; got caught repeatedly,
      and set the goods back down blinking.
      We drank a lot. I paid his way.
      Then, in Detroit, three years ago,
          when I was about
    to leave to take this job, I had listened
      to a man who said, "Father, where
          you go, you'll see cops,

    and cops are tough. You better believe it.
          I used to be
a cop in Akron, in a real neighborhood.
    My buddy on the beat was supposed to stick
          with me, but he had him
      a little piece down there he went
          up to see, so once
      this pair got me alone. One pinned

my arms. The other started cutting, cut my chest,
      shoulders, both cheeks; and I was too scared
      to yell. Then I saw my buddy
      stand ten yards off taking aim, and Thupp!
          the man who cut me
    relaxed, hit square in the head; Thupp! the one
      who held me just relaxed and fell;
          and was I relieved.

27

You better believe it. From the time they
        got me until
they died they never spoke. I had to spend two months
    in the hospital. Then I quit the force fast.
        You better believe it."
    I left that man. I left the bar.
        In the parking lot
    a dozen Syrian or Greek men

were dancing, hand in hand. The lead man waved a scarf.
    They circled, hunched, jumped, then tilted
    on one foot. In front of them Spano
    played the flute. We two talked a while.
        I walked away.
    Spano stayed alone then, wrapped in black, below
    a streetlight, singing. I thought the smoke
        his cigarette

uncoiled poised straight against the wind. Midnight
        and midnight blue.
The guards wear midnight blue in here, and so did Mosh
    at the university. He claimed to be
        embittered by poverty.
    I never saw him poor. He taught
        a seminar,
    though he was just four years my elder,

in Stoicism, I remember. "Learn the truth,"
    he said, "so you can sell your lies,"
    a teacher of philosophies,
    a scholar of mysticism,
        an understander
of antique music and of modern art,
    cognizant of contemporary
        political

ideologies; and he said "Innocence
          does not relate
to truth nor Nature to integrity," and I
     agreed; I agree today. When he retired,
          age thirty-two, I asked
          him where he'd go. He said "I am
               a private soldier
          now, in the class war. Money," he said,

"there's money galore in it." At first he broke strikes.
     I later heard he was a gunman.
     I asked him. He said "I have force,
     expensive force for sale. And what
          goes cheaper than
an intellectual?" And I agreed.
     That was the last I saw of him.
          He can go to Hell.

But what about Hell? How may I believe
          when what I say
perverts itself? I can no more stand steady than
     rescind the primal hate of brother for
          brother. I ought to stand
     with men in blue; or better, men
          in black who wear
     one black for kinship, communing

in contrariety to Nature, manufacture
     of integrity from desire.
     I ought to stand with Mosh and truth,
     or Spano and integrity;
          for I cannot stand
     beside my soulful children, men in grey
          mauled in the eschatological
               ruckus of outside.

Tutti came in today and said he'd sinned.
  Is that the truth?
God's truth. The truth, I said, Has made too many slaves
  already and set none free. He scratched his head.
    Scratching cannot avail,
    I said, When the itching is inside
      your skull. He left.
    And sure enough, an hour after,

Swamp Fox slunk in and said "How do I know I've sinned,
  Father? How do I know for sure?"
    I said Truth flakes and falls. You're lucky
    to be in here. (I guess I napped:
      Father and Mother
    and I are under ground, all of us clad
    in Salvation Army garb. I watch
      the family creep

in mephitic passages. Rocks fall on them.
    So this is Hell.
The loam and stones sag more and more. Somehow I crawl
  into the sun again. I stray into
    a cottage. An old aunt,
    my last relation, putters about
      the kitchen. I saw
    them die, I say. She cuddles me.

"I live mostly with our dead," she says. I walk out.
    I guess you wear that jacket all
    year round, I ask the soft old hound.
    She nuzzles me. Answer yes or no,
      I shout. The dog
  nods yes. And under the jacket do you wear
    a brassiere? No or yes, I ask
      threateningly.

The dog nods yes.) I woke to find Swamp Fox
            still waiting there.
He scratched his head. I said Dandruff was enough. Now you're
    knee deep. *In what?* In wit-flakes. More fall every
            minute. Your categories
        are peeling, son. We prisoners
            of truth must wait
        on the *Weltmoder*; then, supposing

I or you ever do get out of this jail, there'll
        be just enough truth left in our heads
        so that we can take thousand-mile
        bus trips, five a week, reading all
            the roadside signs
    out loud: Reserved for Retarded Children.
        Beware of Falling Rocks. Jesus Saves.
            Chew *Yankee Girl*.

Spano

The hill men descend twice a year. Before
the rains a few come to buy tobacco
and after the rains a hundred or so
pass a weekend camping along the shore.
Thick, black, serious people, having no use
for whites or littoral natives, they wait
in camp and watch the ocean palpitate
as their agents auction the year's produce.

In 1872 a German
philosopher was endowed for three years'
research and he came to these mountaineers
to try a language of perfect reason
he had invented, based on harmony;
and he succeeded—without the applause
however, of the institute, because
his papers were buried with him at sea.

Today it is, I said, Here's the cable.
The river is waning now; tomorrow
our steamer leaves. I awaken Spano.
About noon we approach the hill people.
Skirled through reeds on a gourd resonator,
their solemn discourse fretted spine and skull.
This may be scandalous, I hope not dull,
says Spano, assembling his recorder.
He was twice wrong. Respectfully, sedate,
the hill men receive his baroque music
as an elaborate dialectic
all might attend though few discriminate.

New Day

There, white, like legs of women swimmers sounding, glinted
the humping, dipping sea at noon. While Spano played
Handel allegros on the recorder and largos
on the flute, I poured a whiskey sour and squinted
beyond that glamorous mile: Out of the north a yacht
was being towed toward us. Maybe the sirens made
her crew, I said, So now, like an abandoned wife,
once proud, she lets a vulgar matron lead her. Why not,

said Spano, groping for his gin unsteadily.
That afternoon we slept, until Mijnheer Sardam
arrived, that is, fanning himself. Gentlemen, he said,
Please, come along to help. There's such a mystery,
I can't tell you. Due north of here, eight knots or less,
I found a yacht adrift empty. In Surinam
this will appear incredible. She's two weeks out
of Kingston. Shipshape. There had been no SOS.

Incredible indeed, said Spano, winking slowly.
(We three had boarded her at dusk to avoid moonlight.
By now the moon faded.) Five sailors gone, Spano
continued, Owners gone, why not. The sea is lustful.
We know that here. Here you're an officer. Here you're white.
They'll mention murder down in Paramaribo.
Why not. You'll be just one brown *burger* in that city.
By dawn Sardam had stripped her of all he could budge
except a blowtorch he laid somewhere abaft her,
then thanked us piously. I said it was a trifle.
Toward noon, while Spano slept, I watched a spreading smudge
drift north above the deep waves' numberless laughter.

35

Mosh

Every midnight in the Dream, Mosh the finger-man
    held forth, great-voiced and long of period:
"They say Endymion (shall we believe the tale?)
    fell slumbering (one evening long ago)
on Latmus (a mountain of the East) and I believe
    that no one has thus far awakened him."

"Why need you, Mosh," I said, "a man of serious action,
    whose every labor is irrevocable,
quote Cicero to Spano at the bar? Why lure
    my favorite fool to fatuous paradise?
You don't believe Endymion feels it, do you,
    when the Moon is cold? What does he care?
He doesn't even know. You, Spano, think of that
    these mornings, in corridors where dreams begin."

"Spano is too coarse for the sensual plea," said Mosh.
    "He's gross with music and watching the world pass.
Now he waits, in the lesser hours. A lady comes,
    flickering with alternately quadrifoil
and vermiform tongue, bows, palps him, nibbles the veins.
    To lie asleep a minute more will do."

Mosh spoke true. And what could my valediction be
    when an incremental vision, seen in sleep,
would widow me of the relic of my roving times?
    "Not slumber and unperceived caresses,
but hungry ranging among stones and cypresses
    will come of you, and fittingly," I said,
"while Mosh, who tenders Sensibility, sings other
    companions to your doom, and I grieve those."

Faith

I did my least and best: how about that.
The soul, I heard Mosh claim, is visibly
the size of the half-moon of your thumb nail
but actually (you know?) a good bit smaller.
All right, supposing half of *that* excised,
you can imagine how destroyed a man would be.

I woke before dawn feeling poor. I crawled
out on the fire-escape for air and saw
a union man, then Mosh behind him, like
a quick beetle, break his neck, plant his pockets,
then carry him away, and seeing Mosh I thought
of Spano (who I knew knew him) and I

was worried suddenly. I hurried down.
The door shook open. "Sucked it," said Spano,
"from my neck near the ear." I saw a skirt
or tentacle slip past and ran to follow it,
but all I saw was like a rabbit with
a broken back flop down the stairs (you know?)

and Spano kept saying "She sucked out half,"
and soon he was an idiot. "What can
he do?" I said he played the flute. "We need a flute.
You've done the best thing bringing him. I see
that you have faith." That was at the Shelter.
I asked him what he meant. "You are a man

who waits. The least thing faith can do is wait.
Your friend here waited: do you know now what I mean?
This isn't Heaven. Someday, maybe, off-hand,
you'll follow a non-Euclidean alley
or discover that just a silly membrane
divides you from a different special scene."

How about that. Spano you'll see with an old lady
   Santa Claus, blowing "Silent Night." Meanwhile
   I just wait. I think I'll find a parked car soon,
   and there's a man inside, all pale and streaked
   and soft (you know?) like the white of an eye.
   That's faith for you. I did ask Mosh. Shrugged, smiled.

Santa Monica

What may a childless man perform on the public sands?
I ask of amber seaweed languishing underfoot.
Here, where twice yearly the serious citizens descend
from urban hills to sniff and hug the Pacific,
now, this interim season, nervous sandpipers
are picking the gravel, and gulls go fifing over
the many dead of their kind that arrive in the surf
like goddesses of love. Now I flounder barefoot
along the line of tide, another hunter here,
another mourner too, grubbing for mussel and clam,
sorrowed with moored small yachts and a bell-buoy's moan.

"What is this childish man deriving from dead sand?"
one shouts. Bizarre in blue silk suit, fat, approaching
in glides like a bull sea lion rippling seaward
from alarm, Mosh, holding a Homburg, descends to me.
"Who is this raggedy man with a toy trowel?
What is he doing without a whiskey bottle?"
Each lap of ocean betrays the bubbling of clams.
See how their blow-holes stay as the running sand settles.
(I dig one, not fast enough; another much faster,
a foot deep. Zero.) I belong here, Mosh, I plead.
I hazard an at least innocuous livelihood,

although it's off of what I love: this nape-tan sand
and flank-white foam. I've loved this ocean on both ends.
"To live off what you love," says Mosh, "is childhood's game.
I have lived off what I fought, although on changing sides.
And all the citizens who take a bus and spend
the afternoon or take a cabin to spend the time
they think they've saved that year in the happy nation's
scullery of needful toil are kindred of mine,
serious people in retirement." I am too weak
for greed, I say. But why choose Santa Monica
to rest from murder or hide from a subpoena

when, by now, in Lower California, clear sands
lie warm and the small Gulf brings no sudden messengers?
Mosh says: "There is no difference in obscurity.
I could return a while to a university,
but now too many of my style are concealed there.
For now, I'll make this industrial beach my Baiae,
enjoy its vegetable stench, and let you wimble
your row of fence-post holes to keep away the sounds
of victims the ocean holds. You are sentimental
enough to see men's pulps the rotted water braids
and to hear their bones clatter in the nether tides."

I see that much and more, I say. This is living sand.
It winces with mussels. They call it Muscle Beach,
if you like a joke. You can find wee polyps on black
Pacific stones which, when you prod them, fold their pink
clamps shut. I guess you're paid for silence now. Your nine
years' service has made you discreet as Seneca
or something clinging from the sea. You talk to me
because I am helpless. Look at the playful waves
hopping like puppies the color of guns. This should be
the place for an out-of-season holyman to go
to outshout the pebbles boiling in the undertow.

Palms

Under enormous green-browed palms, a sage,
bearded and sandaled and bald, observes
three brothers in swimsuits turn handsprings and cartwheels.
One of the three is about sixteen,
the others one year and two years younger, the age
most easily and justly sentimentalized.

He is uninterested, though, in shapes—
agile or sensual—that the boys
configurate, and ultimately bored with souls
light or tormented. He leaves to play
catch with others like himself. They resemble apes:
beards to belly and head-hair hanging to their backsides.

Chimps in a carnival playing baseball,
holy fatuity aping youth,
I mutter to Spano who shares my bench. He slobbers,
infantile, over his uniform,
a black Salvation Army coat, and turns a graceful
inverted turn on the flute. One of the sages

offers him sunflower seeds. He trills
thanks to the whisking palmetto fronds,
brushed in ocean wind, that sound like leisured dancers
scrubbing obliquely, heard through sad music.
"Better to nibble a little dry seed than dead swills
you make of creatures you destroy," a hunched form tells me.

"We are an Order, and Spano's our saint."
How may you imitate innocence,
I ask, Except by intolerable misery?
"Feign it directly, grotesque as need be,"
a pithecoid figure says. "No mind means no taint."
Spano pipes a silly tune to this. I stare outward,

listening meanwhile, along the blind
  ocean as green as an eye. Spano,
I say, Is speaking, and you are chumps to believe
  anything spoken so musically
by the holiest fool; for no taint means no mind,
and his music has fallen from its old beauty.

Under enormous blond-bearded palms,
  genuine sages of Santa Monica,
I watch three boys, alone now but for a pederast
  sharing my bench. The ape-men lead Spano
away. He plays the flute. They hum some wordless psalms.
The submerging sun shows pink as a baby's finger.

Three

The Gift

Mine grew a wart, a torment to a mind
fourteen, when imperfection is an insult.
Many days I watched it; many nights bit
the red meat, while with thumb and index gripped
the white wart, but failed each time to pluck it free.
Awful enough only to force it forward.
           What could I do?
fearful of seeing as of showing it,
as though it were that other article
which, without becoming nasty vulgar
or medical nasty, our mother tongue
is unable to name; afraid too to use
a razor, tool I had still far from mastered:
for thus the root of the growth could remain
and might thicken for the lopping and extend
its morbid rhizome slowly till it rose
and strangled me. In those years excess seemed
more harsh and probable a hurt than loss.
I had seen calves' tongues whole at butchers' shops,
and guessed they must reach from deep in the gullet.
I had known wretched children called "tongue tied,"
but the ligature's nature was not explained.
        For a year, I did nothing.
Facts have a way, though—as does talk—of teasing
out fear, even of hacking awe to the stump.
I studied languages and biology.
I learned snakes smell with their forked—though honest—tongues,
and hear with them. (Smell, I still believe. But hear?
Trust that chatter, and what can you deny?
Taste with their ears? Whisper with them? Next thing,
it's drink with what nice English will not mention.)
But snakes' quick tongues will not articulate.
Dry gasps are all they say. Lacking vocal chords,

they can gulp down fat prey. Next year, I joined
chorus and band; learned how my own voice went,
and learned about the flutter-tongue of flutes
and double-tongue of—truthful—trumpeters;
                and, at last, did it.
Twenty years of probable nights and days
have spread, denser always and more rapid,
between today and then. At its root, my tongue
aches with the dread that constricts the throat still;
while the tip is quick with professorial skill.
A friend and I discussed this lately, while—
the hush come, wives gone to the living room,
the three boys, my six and four, his five-year-old,
run to the back to play—I washed, he wiped:
a twenty-minute task between two men,
cheered by deep talk. For, both of us, who lack
the gift of tongues, teach language; both had learned
to bind hiatuses with tangled thought;
and now the tang of wine had left us glib.
We went on: Once I heard a medium,
I told him, speak in tongues; Algonquian,
it sounded. Yes, but then, he said, I heard
a Mexican extemporize in gibberish
that sounded just like English. On we went.
Tibetans, surely, are as fond of seeing
as of showing it. What does this shameless
greeting mean? Mean? "Up and over!" What else?
What are you two doing? Where are the boys?
Twenty minutes had slipped by, plus a hundred.
Each rinsed dish I passed my friend, he polished
then placed back in the suds: this, we discovered
only now. The boys were in the alley.
We rushed first to remove the garbage. Pouring

pots of hot water down the can's inside,
we freed each boy in rising order of age.
They sat in torment, but couldn't raise a sob
among them. In a ritual triangle
they sat, tongues stuck to the receptacle—
no wonder at ten below—by bonds of ice,
wretched as dogs whose unnameable portion
nature's imperfection has detained—or
more wretched. After the early flutter flagged
and the evaded questions had been voided,
pain of frostbite lingered. To cheer the boys,
      I told them what I did.
"Gripping it," I said, "in my incisors,
with an abrupt gulp twitched my tongue back; spat
the lanceolate growth down the bathroom sink,
eradicated; bled two hours after;
tip hurt three days. The trick I learned from that was
to treat mouth matters in and with the mouth."
They slept. I said, "No excess here, in fact.
For them, the tongue has by now begun to be
an instrument of conquest." We left it there.
But, since we still sat, I could not withhold
addenda: We were about their age then.
A group of English children and their teachers
were conducted through the Cairo museum.
They reached the case where Ramses lies unwrapped.
They gaped. The guide—when the Pharaoh sat up—ran.
The jaw dropped. Some children ran. The teachers
explained. Then the stiff, black tongue was extended,
quivered; and there was heard a guttural,
dry gasp. The children all ran. Some were trampled.
The world turned. Awful fear, as solid as
the polished plate displayed, as sturdy as

the spears racked there, choked the frozen teachers.
The Pharaoh continued to try to speak,
maybe to say at last "You stupid, vulgar,
shameless, tongue-tied Jew! A pox on you, Moses,
and on your sprouting staff! Plague me no more.
Our ears are weary of this nastiness.
Please mention it no further. Show him the door."

Niagara

Mist-moist, past the rainbow, we make a small row
    at the low wall on the Canadian side:
you, and the other, who, as we approached the roar,
    often and oftener groped your shoulder,
and I, a stranger almost, along for the ride.

    Hundreds of soulful strangers, high
on the speedy water in their bodies,
    lean on this rail, couples, eyes full or floating,
        and all of them narcotized
    unawares, by the falls, through the eye,
as veritably as by the needle
        they despise and call sinful.

Apart from you two by two yards, I scan
    the American side for the rapids
I already know; see them as a harum-scarum
    taffeta cancan seesawing in sunlight,
now higgledy-piggledy the grey then white shreds

    shown then withdrawn in the sexy
wingding; and parted from you two and from
    the hundreds by the absence of love in me
        (replaced by a drug), I hear
    that other's chitchat you answer curtly
often and oftener shrill over the falls'
        singsong, and hear in it pain

which I can not respect. Inspecting the falls
    itself at its summit, I see a vein
of the river split on stone then mend, now folding, next
    unfolding until both blend in the mist;
and to you, who have left the other to his pain

momentarily, and his camera,
and have come near me, I liken the white
currents to a groin and she-thighs widening
and clenching. You disagree.
I watch further. I feel Niagara
fill my head through the crown and through my eyes.
Soon, spilling out my mouth

with breath, it returns; encircles my mind;
builds silence. Flowing glee impels me to fall.
To fall, I mount the rail. Suddenly, in unison
with my own thought, you shout *It liquefies me!*
I come down. *Yes, yes,* I tell you. The other, cool,

gripping your shoulder, leads you again
past the rainbow, under sobering mist.
I follow. Later I tell you both both
my own story (how I
am free of love through medicine)
and theorize about the hundreds there
high on love and water.

Safe where Niagara is almost hidden
and merely a moist whirr reveals its action,
we two juggle the topic literarily.
The third, unsure, shuffles picture postcards.
In the park, near the car, in expectation

of franker words in privacy,
I ask again. I hear you, a blur, naming
a seminary where, at dawn, you would run
in pairs or by fours, downwards,
swung to a circular valley,
hills of daisies, grey and white folds, low, up,
lower, to swim secretly.

Ties That Bind

Maybe I'm like one of these people:
I won't tell you which. Why should I tell you?
    You'll know it all one day, in the end,
    I mean the definitive end snap
when the dunnage of the brain is blown out
    and terrible barrels tumble
    in the belly of it, spilling nails.

All of this should have been in a city,
or a seaport settlement for people who dress light.
    Here was Central Texas, however,
    a hundred and more miles from any port,
where I had strayed to avoid water and await
    payments on a twenty years' pension
    to start to allow something like a choice.
And far from warm and trailing negligee, the town

    strung its lazy slivers insanely
the night I arrived, raining cold and dense,
    so that toads emerged in the dark
    and squatted on sidewalks, big toads
whose flat eyes flared in the beams of cars passing;
    and the town stripped, not leaf by leaf,
    but tree by tree in flashes: fig leaves.

An ambiguous autumn, even for me
who had known no climates so long but watery ones.
    I'd have liked traditional first-frosts
    to follow the fall, something to return
me to the bonds of traditional youth: Thanksgiving;
    Christmas; sallow elm leaves that break clean
    and often will wrench off an inch of twig
and more along into space, one by one. Christmas,

though, in Texas terrifies, not as
a perilous thing—as a shapeless one,
   soft, hesitant. Nighthawks scamper
   under the shrubs in bright afternoon,
silly as fish, stub tails and long wings useless.
   Mistletoe lets the oaks seem green still;
   its berries are frozen gouts of cream.

What will a dismal loner do but escape
from what he can? at least from leafy tourbillions
   bursting underfoot and the slime of
   the trodden and drenched leaves as dumb as mud.
Until you know the ropes, a beer joint's the best place.
   You may well go deaf if you listen
   to lies, I've been told. Well, I have been deaf.
Not any longer. These days, I trust every stranger.

Lying's nonexistent. You try it
yourself for a time. Then you'll understand.
   Listen to guys in bars. The one thing
   you'll never hear is lies. Believe me.
I sat beside this fellow—a truck driver
   by trade, but now a pipeliner—
   in a row of mostly buckeroos.

The beer runs; and for reasons of his own
his history begins to open. *Take care,* we say.
   Think of people showing their heirlooms
   to everyone new. They don't take much care.
It all starts out: 'Neighbor, I've got a problem for you.
   How long will it take a one-legged
   grasshopper to kick all the seeds out of
a watermelon?' The other man, the pipeliner,

answers, poking me with his elbow,
"A hell of a while. Even longer time
 than you could hold a hot goose-turd
 in your mouth without slobbering."
Afterward, he told me: "You know how I
 became an alcoholic? Way back
 when I was a baby not weaned yet,

my mother was weak and losing weight fast;
so the doctor they had said she needed nourishment
 she could swallow easy and often.
 So what he prescribed was a goodly tot
of Guinness stout with an egg yolk whipped up in it,
 a pint every morning and bedtime,
 and later at noon also. All the while
she was nursing me she had alcohol inside.

Reason for my alcoholism."
I saw him again. This time several friends
 of the manager were talking
 about the dead. 'You all remember
So and so? Used to come in here Fridays,
 wore cowboy clothes?' "Yes, I believe
 I do." 'Well, he died last month and still's

not been claimed. He's downtown in the deep-freeze.'
"Didn't he have any family ties hereabouts?"
 'Sure he did. What difference does that make?
 If you will recall, Porter Talman stayed
down there a year or more, till finally some cousin
 out of Waco claimed him and took him.
 His sister, who lives right in San Antone,
wouldn't have anything to do with him, live or dead.'

55

Then my friend, who'd heard it before, said
'It's true, every word. What can you expect
    when even wedlock isn't sacred?'
    I answered that I wouldn't know.
'Then listen,' he said, brushing my coat sleeve
    and making that benedictory
    gesture of the palm that drunks make,

'Listen. I used to live up in your part
of the country, in Massachusetts. My work then was
    driving trucks. Two-hundred and fifty
    a week if not more. I was married; had
the sweetest little daughter only five years old.
    Driving's hard. So after the work day,
    the boys always passed, say, a couple hours
drinking beer before heading home. I went with them.

    Sometimes I'd stay late, and my wife said
You stop or I'll leave. I said Driving's hard.
    A man needs something to relax on
    before he's fit to talk to people.
So she said, Okay, from now on you come
    straight home and I'll buy beer for you.
    And that's the way it went for a time.

One night, I'm drinking a little bit, not drunk
exactly, and playing gin rummy with my daughter:
    smartest little thing. I was letting
    her win, for the fun, but she's really fine
at it. Soon my wife walks in the room where we were
    just as she yells Gin! and my wife says
    Your daddy is drunk, go on up to bed.
I couldn't stand for that. I wasn't drunk, either.

Even if I was, though, I told her,
she shouldn't have said things like that in front
of the girl. You know what I did?
I up and walked out then and there.
I put my coat on and cut out and never
came back and never heard from them.
My daughter should be sixteen now.'

I exited; shuffled on sidewalks, stumbling
where the walks idiosyncratically ended.
Wind-whipped Yule insignia, fixed on
municipal lamps, hissed like Mexicans.
Even in these fripperies I could find no falsehood:
not in kissing sounds of my shoe-soles
or brushing of drenched creatures in the shrubs.
I was not prepared to deny phenomena.

Much detachment challenges people's
resources. Time melts. Novelty's the thing.
Leaving my shoes in the foyer,
I assumed sandals. A Hindu
beanery in the center of Texas!
Novelty's the only recourse.
A reed portiere, strung with bells, blared

as I parted it. A tapestried chamber,
with three woven-straw tables and pillows for seats:
at the farthest table a young man
was squatting in gloom, reading half aloud.
I sat near the door. A couple girls took the center
seat and started whispering. Food came.
A Chinaman served, kneeling silently
beside each table, withdrawing like a dancer,

57

barefoot. Time goes fluid with strangeness.
The voice becomes firm. I could hear the girls'
talk now; and the young man, I saw,
began to listen also. One girl
says: 'Here I go again. More calories.
Look at me. My God, when I think
I'm twenty I can't believe it.'

And the other: "I know how you must feel.
All tied up in knots inside. That's how I was at first.
Then I thought I'd better take hold of
myself for the child's sake if nothing else."
'That's all right for you to say. You had a better chance.'
"I did all I could for my husband.
I put him through school, earning every cent
we had the whole time." 'How old is Freddy now? Two?'

"Two last month. My former was here for
the party I had. We get on just fine
these days. Why be bitter? When he
got his A.B. finally, I simply
decided it was time to cut the cord.
And that's the whole thing: discipline."
'That's okay but I just can't bear

that empty feeling inside: down here, you know.
My first would be four now and the second near two.
I can't say I'm sorry, exactly.
The first one I was. Nothing else to do,
or so it seemed. The last two weren't my idea.'
While they spoke, the fellow I mentioned
as sunken in gloom looked about to cry.
Well, well, I thought. Obscure causation is affording

me a lesson. What's the connection?
But tragedy paused. From the kitchen came
    the manager, wearing a kind
    of gymnast's uniform. He bows
to the girls. —Everything all right? (They nod.)
    —I would like to inform you all
    of the course we teach here, at night,

    in Yoga diet and exercise. *Yoga*,
you know, is from the Sanskrit, meaning "a yoking."
    This refers to yoking the body
    and mind by a strict regimen of both
physical and spiritual discipline. "There now,"
    says the second girl to the fat one,
    "That's just what you need." Then the Yogi says
—Of course. From a simple reducing problem we might

    easily proceed to a higher,
    more basic approach. We, you know, are strict
    vegetarians, which has the double
    advantage of improving the soul—
    because no living thing dies so we may live—
    and the body. Vegetables aren't
    fattening or binding, still less

    when Yoga exercise is practiced. Look . . .
(At this moment the manager pulls up his shirt,
    shows his fibrous abdomen to them.)
    . . . not one bit of fat. Look at this control!
(He squeezes the muscles together in the middle.
    With a thoughtful stare he then wiggles
    the muscular bunch like a pendulum.)
But, promising to return, the girls pay and leave.

Soon a second gentleman entered.
He went to the first, younger man, who sulked
   at the far table, and who now
   said 'What's the occasion? Wearing
a tie! and cufflinks; too much! It's fantastic.'
   The other tells him "Got to go
   up to Dallas and see the Judge.

I'm going to explain my wife won't let me see
our boy." 'I don't see the connection, man. Explain.'
   "Nonsupport. She's hollering. I'll just
   remind him that what we agreed to was
I should pay and she should let me visit each month.
   Well, she hasn't." 'Terrible. Going
   in circles. That's love. Don't think I don't know.
Will the circle be unbroken . . .' "What do you know?

You were married only six months and
no children besides. You don't have the right
   to talk about it. We were married
   for six years. No comparison."
'Comparison? I'm sorry, man, but here:
   we're talking absolutes. Love's love,
   if you can't say anything more

you can say that; and man, what does it mean,
divorce or death, or a minute or a golden
   anniversary?' There was silence
   between them a time. Then the older man
says "I'll just have to cash my bonds in." More silence.
   "Sorry I cut loose at you. I was
   abrupt, I admit." 'Doesn't matter, man.
Everyone does what he has to. I think I'll split.'

"No, don't go, not yet. I was thinking.
Forget it. You know, some years back, I had
    a sister-in-law, a lovely girl.
    We all thought a good deal of her:
one of the family, and all the rest of it.
    Well, my brother was a flier.
    He always said when he had to go

he'd want it to happen neat: up there, and all
the rest of it. And it did: a pocket or draught,
    something of that sort that you read of.
    My sister-in-law, well, it was a year,
you know, and all the rest, but it really hurt us,
    worst of all my Pappy, as she was
    a favorite of his. Man she married was
a friend of my brother's and mine." The younger man

    answers, 'Now I see why you're all strung
out. Love, like I said. Man, it's too damn much.
    Like a hole as big as your lungs
    with all kinds of freaks loping through
and out of it when you try to yell names.
    Fantastic. Every time I think
    of that chick it begins tumbling;

and like razorblades spill out in my skull.'
They left together. The bells rang. I waited out
    their reverberation—that like the
reports of a truth dismally hung on
among the leisurely slivers of the portiere
    (so I thought)—then exited into
    the winter of mid-Texas, rain and dark.
It was bound to have happened. That was last week. Tonight

61

I got out of Texas. I think of
my picture of home, Pennsylvania, years
   remote in a humble town where
   the only recreation between
school and dinner was the so-called Cultural
   Hall that the local Bund promoted.
   I remember melodies from then,

  and home in the parlor, whistling and watching
veritable pictures my parents had done. Father
   painted black: a field in the evening,
   the trees silhouettes; unexplained sun rays
from over the trees standing in a meadow like
   women trailing lace, whether golden
   or yellowed with age; or a yard and mill:
stubby forms with burdens treading the frosty mud.

   Pictures by my mother inclined to
be grey. There were reeds, grasses, fragile birch,
   and a brook rippling in a curve,
   like a country road on the parlor
wall, soon beyond sight into another
   dimension; lonely and shy, but sure
   to prove imperious once followed.

I think too of other lonesome intervals
ashore, that terrify and define as well; times as
   lazy and as hesitant, raining
   as faintly as grief, blended into one
dream of fog and walking, shoe-suck on soaked cement,
   seeking to remember the words of
   Brahms' "Lullaby," can't, so confuse it with
a song of Mozart that goes *Schlaf ein, meine Prinzchen.*

Strangers, shocked, would flash at me flat eyes,
ambiguously full of afterhope
    for what I could not have fathomed,
    and their very flatness disguised.
Loners, like stripped trees, like catamarans
    split into separate hulls, silly
    and useless, I usually thought.

Home is where the heart is. For me, that was
the sea, salty as sweat, with hundreds of fellows
    bound by nothing less than an ocean
    or more than a job. There's no privacy,
but no privation either. Buddies of mine who know
    tell me it's the same in a prison.
You're glad to get out; glad to get back too.
Because home is where the heart is, and the heart is

    like a rope or ligament, nothing
but something between. So, I'm going back,
    not to the sea, but to people.
    A buddy wrote me there's a nice
tea shop for lease up in Eastern Michigan.
    My pension's come through, and I'm only
    forty-four. I can keep long hours.

Nice talking to you. Got another train
to catch. Good-bye St. Louis. No thanks, there's no time.
    Yes, I thought today that the force that
    sets stems in their place has itself a cause
that is caused, and so on forever. The arcs join,
    mend a circle. We are upon it.
    The circle, like us, has a memory.
Maybe you're like one of those too. Happy New Year!

Against Nature

To combat
nature, not man,
is what men do which is most concordant
with nature. Supposing
this, I have no choice: I conjure ancient
Greek, compose verse,
and (my one
recreation) lift weights.

This is why,
negatively,
I will not speak Russian, or make speeches
or even play handball.
What snobbery this is. Humanity,
variable,
unstable,
missing that dignity

of repose
the feeblest bug
manifests—what presumption to proclaim
the belief that only
time, probability, and gravity
merit human
enmity,
that is, my own effort.

Presuming,
as I seem to,
that a sort of Heaven is in the pith
of us, to be attained
by, so to speak, defoliation, like
an artichoke,
then both hope
and loss are reckoned scars.

You perceive
traces of such
pride in children too—but disorderly,
not composed by mercy—
and in chickens: both depraved, both enslaved.
Picking, tearing,
and snapping
in differing rhythms,

caponed cocks
cooped close until
obese, hens stimulated by night lights
till their eggs run with blood,
and white geese, fettered with twine, fed by force
till one liver
swells so big
it fills a coffee can:

none of these,
by an insult
accidental to our language all called
"fowl" or "poultry," can fly;
still, they all try to, dinning paltry wings
to no result.
Of children,
more will be said shortly.

Now, seated
beneath a tree-
-of-Heaven, a growth common in alleys
beside blackened brick walls
of Detroit, here by the corner of my
Y.M.C.A.
closest to
the boys' entrance, I watch

               a boy kneel
              to reach his knee,
      where a bandage, white as one convulsing
              wing of a large cabbage-
butterfly from which three wings have been torn,
              flaps in rhythm
              with his thumb
              with which he picks a scab,

              the fibers
              of which are so
dense with time that the prime red has turned black.
              This picture, magnified
      by fatigue, I must (made meditative
              with fatigue) match
              with the form
              and unsolicited

              confession
              of a fellow
      weightlifter: a lad with a thick back, short
              forearms, but a total
      loss in Olympic lifting because of
              a hopeless knee,
              injury
              sustained playing football.

              "I can't split
              or squat," he said
      "The tendon's been cut out." He kneeled half way
              to show a four inch white
      scar on his right leg, the leg you go back
              on to clean and
              jerk. Said next
              (and here the kid in him

came right out)
"I can't even
keep good calluses on my hands. I pick
them off." Soon a second
lifter entered, a heavyweight, a man
nearly fifty,
about whom
more must be said shortly.

I believe
something native
in us takes joy in clicks and snaps—the act
of stripping, of plucking,
shredding and husking things; act, not purpose—
and that children
most widely
demonstrate that this joy

must be had.
Dandelions
are just right. First in spring, to click the stem
loose, clasp it, aim the gold
head then shoot it somewhere with a thumb-flip;
next in summer,
pucker lips
then toot the concentric

parachutes
off everywhere
(recompense, perhaps, for spring ravages).
Also in summer comes
the tree-of-Heaven, this tree here, with fronds
as great as twelve
or fifteen
pairs of leaves plus one leaf,

and of as
little as five
pairs and no tip-leaf (arrogant pivot
of symmetry); fronds which,
dropping continually to earth, are
grasped at the base
by children
who begin at the base

and with thumb
and two fingers
run the leaves off in one quick jerk, tempoed,
for all its brevity,
by the tiny poppings of leaf-stems clean
from the frond-stem,
sensed by hands
with pleasure, true pleasure.

The stripped frond
is utilized,
in the fall of the year, as a saber,
to whack corpuscle-shaped
grey seeds of hollyhocks, crisply, from their
circular pods.
The rule holds
in manufactured goods

equally.
Children prefer
a father's cast-off golfballs to handballs,
not only for simple
bouncing but for baseball-against-the-steps.
The black handball,
efficient
as it is, is too smooth,

integral,
and unaging;
but the worn golfball's white shell will at last
split and may be husked then,
the dark brown inside unravelled, a yards-
long rubber band,
till the core,
a mystic pocket-piece,

is attained,
soon to be lost.
I am not expert in the symbolic
values of juveniles.
Still, I imagine the pleasure I had
an hour ago
in the gym
is not excessively

deviant
from the joy had
from scabs, leaves, and calluses. I loaded
the bar, *clink, clink,* higher
than I'd ever tried. Chalked my hands up. Gazed
at those black plates
(like the seeds
of hollyhocks) and white

chalk-splotches
left where I'd changed
grips. Breathed. Cleaned it with much difficulty.
Breathed up again, scared. Dipped,
and heaved it to eye height. My right foot slid,
the left knee gave,
but then *wham,*
a click, and I had it,

and, knees locked,
held it. I left
the platform, heading for the shower, when
this man, the heavyweight
I mentioned, stopped me. We stood in the main
hall where the din
of handball
combined of several courts

was channeled
from a smaller
hall and poured out to us. He told me how
forty summers ago
in the vacation tedium of age
eight, he and some
other boys,
toyless, bookless, sexless,

had tied down
and wetted down
some geese and chickens, and plucked them as clean
as for the oven, then
freed them in an abandoned barn. "All those
feathers," he said,
"Just as white
as waitresses' dresses.

What damn things
kids do sometimes."
And I said Heaven's their aim. Like stripping
an antique sentence down,
or clicking out a line, or snapping up
a large barbell.
It's a proud
combat against nature,

71

the insults
of confinement. . . .
Naturally, the man didn't disagree
or agree, or even
respond. He jerked his thumb toward the next hall
and said "You hear
those handballs?
That's what they sounded like."

The Oil

Waiting for someone to die
(this is the seventh day
of the presumptive death)

I think of you I love
(in your perilous life
so dishonestly led

through consequences of
prior dishonest acts)
to strengthen flabby hours

of waiting with other impatient members of the vigil
who like me insist to themselves: *Let her be dead finally
or recover at last to let us make up our minds at once
about what to think for a while and what to feel for a while.*

From the carpeted waiting room
I watch the city swarm regardless
of April wind that squeals like babies
and wets the canopy of the bar

where earlier tonight I listened
to people talk, a locomotive
trumpeting (and the wet wind curved
that tone then scraped it on corners

of buildings while those people talked
and somebody obscure blew tenor).
*For minor aches or you're going to die,
either, you call a healer, but don't*

*for infection. How's that now? A stroke's
the worst there is going; call straightway,
you can't lose. Now the soul's tough, the
toughest thing there is going. How's that?*

And now I return to the watch down the hall, Ella Lou,
regarded askance and smelled by the other visitors,
and with them watch one whom I love, a painter in oil,
                                        appear
now in the form of a turbaned face inside a fluttering
cellophane membrane full of oxygen, which face lets honking
noises, makes fish-mouths like soulful kisses lusting on air,
as blood bubbles from the nose and the cheeks maintain a
                                        flapping.

> Along this deadly spring as along a string
> I hark to spring a year ago, Ella Lou,
> when another transfiguring death grew
> abruptly out of nothing but the land,
> which planted with nothing yields nothingness.

> This face I watch resembles mine, estranged
> with disease and time. Resemblance has been
> a factor of love before. And change, in
> the earth, is alienating the love
> of a year ago in unflattering ways.

> This has been a painter in oil who stretched
> oil thin as tempera into hazy
> ponds and thin lotuses, living sixty
> years tense and tenuously as her livid
> art, by codeine, benzedrine, her own kindness.

> That other has been painted in oil, destroyed,
> inhumed, in maybe thirty years all told
> in which none (and we were several) was bold
> enough to have discovered how the lonely
> soil of her lay bare and yelling for (who knows?)

one of us, all of us. Meeting on streets,
in offices, halls, often, the wedding band,
or her look that a touch would wound her hand,
or white-rayed black hair, spider-webbed, that left
me a hint of some doom but not neediness

deferred my proffering coffee or sympathy or what
I should have offered, what we wished all to offer, always.
In the end, spring came. On the highest hill of that city,
a sanitarium. She, on the seventh, the highest level
of it stood hearing, I know, the wind falling like babies
around the ledges. Below, in the steepest valley in town,
she saw the married veterans' tenements. Beyond, the relic
of a forest; surrounding that, the graveyard, nourishing it.
Lovers, the first of those the season makes, in refuge there.
Moles, voles; nudging roots, jostling thistles. Between parked
                                        cars she struck
with the sound of a shot, bounced, curled up, slackened,
                                        trembled, stopped.

In what we name final I see no finality,
        no more than what there is original
is discernible to me in any origin.
        If birth is the cause of death, death is that
of birth, absolutely, and spring a year ago
        did not surprise me by becoming winter.

Downtown went swarming over softening ice, under
        a wet snowfall, southward toward the jammed river.
December gusts, forced colder than the standing air,
        swerved into us, hustled us, screwed the noise
of bells and saxhorns and scratched it against parked cars.
        Despairing, I retired to a saloon.

75

Maybe you know it, Ella Lou. Skip the name. Next door
    to one burlesque show, in front of another;
the lonesome burlesque types hang out there, and some girls.
    I drank my gin, dried my glasses, listened
to talk, looked at the Tom & Jerry cauldron, saw
    a ring of holly then a sort of window.

Under a cellophane duster lay a mixture
    of oil and dirt, a painting; and appearing
in that form was she who had died: glowing, smiling,
    hands linked behind her neck, the right nipple,
flat, balancing her bright right eye, left eye unseen,
    the left nipple seen in profile erect.

Each time the door was swung, a gulp of noise entered,
    traffic and carols; between times, the rising
speech of the girls. *Down on the beach at Acapulco,*
    and that's a beach, long, white, smooth, warm, there was
a lot of other girls besides us. There was one
    other girl who was from San Francisco,

and there was a good-looking like dark, muscular
    Mexican boy there, about fifteen, wearing
rose swim-tights, and this girl says He's like Christ at twelve,
    and so this other girl, from San Francisco
also, says How do you know? Any place you can
    dance till 5:30 in the morning's okay.

That's what I like about Acapulco. But it's
    not like that there anymore. It's something new:
1:30 a.m. Is that for sure? Afterward,
    in the bus for home, Ella Lou, the oil,
which had heaped its archaic luminance into me,
    reminded me first of my discoveries

of the progress of our beginning love caressing me
with changes day to day like a drink of gin, reminded
me second of the alienating changes of her
by then, beside a shrunken wood, below the weighty loam.
At first full flesh resists. Wait a little. Feel it. Wait. Now
the finger-dent is slow in filling. Soon it will not fill.
The lungs fold. Veins clog. Curves narrow. Fat runs and
water rises.
What can escape will escape. The brain is sealed in its
chamber.
In secret in the honeycombs in her quiet bones their shape
remains to only the stiffest cells. The marrow shrivels.
What could escape has secretly done so. Her hair abides.

Now in dwindling hours we are observing
the bed and the shape on the bed
as though awaiting a transfiguration,
an emergence like the double
exposure of cinema, that will let
us wince and offer sympathy.

But what will her motions be that will change us
from eager fear to that smug shame?
I alone here feel it will not differ from
my vision of other beds where,
stricken, bouncing, curled up, slackening, shaking,
still, were you, whom I owe kindness.

I think of you I love, whose beauty is
invulnerability, and think
that she I loved had had such beauty too,
and could never have been destroyed
but for the obscure painter in oil who
in love had duplicated her.

77

I think of you whose hands and face are (now,
  to me) the memory of the color
of a cloud, and think my love can never
  so arrogantly define and kill.
So I alone among many here wait
  fearless of resemblance and of change.

By and by, Ella Lou, I shall join you
    in unclassified love,
  like mice in the thistles (by your
    fantastic dishonesty,

on a heap of stolen carpets) when thin
    prior sunlight circles
  the false blue of your clenched morning
    eyes like an absurd ring

of babies hand in hand spinning in the air.
    Hair will hold to kisses,
  over and over: it is an
    anonymous principle.

I watch the shadow of your knee, fluffy
    in its halos of paler
  shadow, amalgamate, through and through,
    on the wall, with the firmer

shadow of my back: an anonymous
    consequence, Louella,
  Ella Lou, like that by which I must
    never presume to learn

you in an altered love so luminously
    that a definitive
  cross can be smeared (by me, by someone)
    against your lying name.

DATE DUE
